# EASY ITALIAN COOKBOOK

## AUTHENTIC ITALIAN COOKING

By
Chef Maggie Chow
Copyright © 2015 by Saxonberg Associates

Published by
BookSumo, a division of Saxonberg Associates
http://www.booksumo.com/

# INTRODUCTION

Welcome to *The Effortless Chef Series*! Thank you for taking the time to download the *Easy Italian Cookbook*. Come take a journey with me into the delights of easy cooking. The point of this cookbook and all my cookbooks is to exemplify the effortless nature of cooking simply.

In this book we focus on Italian. You will find that even though the recipes are simple, the taste of the dishes is quite amazing.

So will you join me in an adventure of simple cooking? If the answer is yes (and I hope it is) please consult the table of contents to find the dishes you are most interested in. Once you are ready jump right in and start cooking.

— Chef Maggie Chow

# TABLE OF CONTENTS

# ANY ISSUES? CONTACT ME

If you find that something important to you is missing from this book please contact me at maggie@booksumo.com.

I will try my best to re-publish a revised copy taking your feedback into consideration and let you know when the book has been revised with you in mind.

: )

— Chef Maggie Chow

# LEGAL NOTES

# COMMON ABBREVIATIONS

| cup(s) | C. |
|--------|-----|
| tablespoon | tbsp |
| teaspoon | tsp |
| ounce | oz. |
| pound | lb |

*All units used are standard American measurements

# Chapter 1: Easy Italian Recipes

## Authentic Italian Antipasto

### Ingredients

- 4 C. diced cauliflower
- 4 C. pearl onions
- 2 C. diced red bell peppers
- 2 C. diced green bell peppers
- 2 C. diced celery
- 2 cucumbers - peeled, seeded and diced
- 2 C. carrots, diced
- 2 C. vegetable oil
- 2 C. distilled white vinegar
- 1 (6 oz.) can tomato paste
- 1 tbsp pickling spice, wrapped in cheesecloth
- 1 C. black olives
- 1 C. pitted green olives
- 4 C. canned mushrooms
- 1 1/2 (6 oz.) cans tuna, drained and flaked

### Directions

- Get a bowl, combine: cucumbers, cauliflower, celery, pearl onions, and bell peppers.
- Submerge the mix in water and salt and let everything sit for 10 hrs.
- Get a 2nd bowl for your carrots and let the carrots sit submerged in salt water for the same amount of time as well.

- Now get the following boiling: pickling spice, veggie oil, tomato paste, and vinegar.
- Once the mix is boiling add in the carrots after draining them.
- Let the veggies cook for 12 mins.
- Now drain the cucumber mix and add these veggies to the boiling carrots.
- Let everything continue to cook for 12 more mins.
- Combine in: the tuna, black olives, mushrooms, and green olives.
- Stir the mix then shut the heat.
- Now throw away the pickling spice and place everything in storage containers.
- Enjoy.

Amount per serving (56 total)

Timing Information:

| Preparation | 1 h |
|---|---|
| Cooking | 30 m |
| Total Time | 9 h 30 m |

Nutritional Information:

| Calories | 102 kcal |
|---|---|
| Fat | 8.5 g |
| Carbohydrates | 5.1g |
| Protein | 2.1 g |
| Cholesterol | 1 mg |
| Sodium | 168 mg |

* Percent Daily Values are based on a 2,000 calorie diet.

# CLASSICAL ALFREDO

## Ingredients

- 6 skinless, boneless chicken breast halves - cut into cubes
- 6 tbsps butter, divided
- 4 cloves garlic, minced, divided
- 1 tbsp Italian seasoning
- 1 lb fettuccini pasta
- 1 onion, diced
- 1 (8 oz.) package sliced mushrooms
- 1/3 C. all-purpose flour
- 1 tbsp salt
- 3/4 tsp ground white pepper
- 3 C. milk
- 1 C. half-and-half
- 3/4 C. grated Parmesan cheese
- 8 oz. shredded Colby-Monterey Jack cheese
- 3 roma (plum) tomatoes, diced
- 1/2 C. sour cream

## Directions

- Stir your chicken after coating it with Italian seasoning in 2 tbsp of butter with 2 pieces of garlic.
- Stir fry the meat until it is fully done then place everything to the side.
- Now boil your pasta in water and salt for 9 mins then remove all the liquids.

- At the same time stir fry your onions in 4 tbsp of butter along with the mushrooms and 2 more pieces of garlic.
- Continue frying the mix until the onions are see-through then combine in your pepper, salt, and flour.
- Stir and cook the mix for 4 mins. Then gradually add in your half and half and the milk, while stirring, until everything is smooth.
- Combine in the Monterey and parmesan and let the mix cook until the cheese has melted then add the chicken, sour cream, and tomatoes.
- Serve your pasta topped liberally with the chicken mix and sauce.
- Enjoy.

Amount per serving (8 total)

Timing Information:

| Preparation | 30 m |
|---|---|
| Cooking | 30 m |
| Total Time | 1 h |

Nutritional Information:

| Calories | 673 kcal |
|---|---|
| Fat | 30.8 g |
| Carbohydrates | 57g |
| Protein | 43.3 g |
| Cholesterol | 133 mg |
| Sodium | 1386 mg |

* Percent Daily Values are based on a 2,000 calorie diet.

# EASY ITALIAN PARMIGIANA

Ingredients

- 1 egg, beaten
- 2 oz. dry bread crumbs
- 2 skinless, boneless chicken breast halves
- 3/4 (16 oz.) jar spaghetti sauce
- 2 oz. shredded mozzarella cheese
- 1/4 C. grated Parmesan cheese

Directions

- Coat a cookie sheet with oil then set your oven to 350 degrees before doing anything else. Get a bowl and add in your eggs.
- Get a 2nd bowl and add in your bread crumbs.
- Coat your chicken first with the eggs then with the bread crumbs.
- Lay your pieces of chicken on the cookie sheet and cook them in the oven for 45 mins, until they are fully done.
- Now add half of your pasta sauce to a casserole dish and lay in your chicken on top of the sauce.
- Place the rest of the sauce on top of the chicken pieces. Then add a topping of parmesan and mozzarella over everything.
- Cook the parmigiana in the oven for 25 mins. Enjoy.

Amount per serving (2 total)

Timing Information:

| Preparation | 30 m |
|---|---|
| Cooking | 1 h |
| Total Time | 1 h 30 m |

Nutritional Information:

| Calories | 528 kcal |
|---|---|
| Fat | 18.3 g |
| Carbohydrates | 44.9g |
| Protein | 43.5 g |
| Cholesterol | 184 mg |
| Sodium | 1309 mg |

* Percent Daily Values are based on a 2,000 calorie diet.

# Maggie's Favorite Pasta

## Ingredients

- 2 tbsps olive oil
- 1 anchovy fillet
- 2 tbsps capers
- 3 cloves minced garlic
- 1/2 C. dry white wine
- 1/4 tsp dried oregano
- 1 pinch red pepper flakes, or to taste
- 3 C. crushed Italian (plum) tomatoes
- salt and ground black pepper to taste
- 1 pinch cayenne pepper, or to taste
- 1 (7 oz.) can oil-packed tuna, drained
- 1/4 C. diced fresh flat-leaf parsley
- 1 (12 oz.) package spaghetti
- 1 tbsp extra-virgin olive oil, or to taste
- 1/4 C. freshly grated Parmigiano-Reggiano cheese, or to taste
- 1 tbsp diced fresh flat-leaf parsley, or to taste

## Directions

- Stir fry your capers and anchovies in olive oil for 4 mins then combine in the garlic and continue frying the mix for 2 more mins.

- Now add: pepper flakes, white wine, and orange.
- Stir the mix and turn up the heat.
- Let the mix cook for 5 mins before adding the tomatoes and getting the mix to a gentle simmer.
- Once the mix is simmering add in: cayenne, black pepper, and salt.
- Set the heat to low and let everything cook for 12 mins.
- Now begin to boil your pasta in water and salt for 10 mins then remove all the liquids and leave the noodles in the pan.
- Combine the simmering tomatoes with the noodles and place a lid on the pot. With a low level of heat warm everything for 4 mins.
- When serving your pasta top it with some Parmigiano-Reggiano, parsley, and olive oil.
- Enjoy.

Amount per serving (4 total)

Timing Information:

| Preparation | 20 m |
|---|---|
| Cooking | 35 m |
| Total Time | 55 m |

Nutritional Information:

| Calories | 619 kcal |
|---|---|
| Fat | 17.7 g |
| Carbohydrates | 79.5g |
| Protein | 31.2 g |
| Cholesterol | 14 mg |
| Sodium | 706 mg |

* Percent Daily Values are based on a 2,000 calorie diet.

# Lasagna Bakes

## Ingredients

- 8 whole wheat lasagna noodles
- 1/2 lb ground turkey
- 6 cloves garlic, crushed
- 1 (10 oz.) package frozen diced spinach, thawed and drained
- 1/2 C. diced fresh chives
- 1/2 tsp dried oregano
- 1/2 tsp dried parsley
- 1/4 tsp dried basil
- 2 egg whites
- 1 (15 oz.) container reduced-fat ricotta cheese
- 2 tbsps crumbled low-fat feta cheese
- 2 tbsps grated Parmesan cheese
- 1/2 tsp ground black pepper
- 1 (28 oz.) jar low-fat tomato pasta sauce
- 1/2 C. shredded low-fat Cheddar cheese

## Directions

- Set your oven to 375 degrees before doing anything else.
- Boil your pasta in water and salt for 9 mins then remove all the liquids.
- Begin to stir fry your garlic and turkey for 12 mins and break the meat into pieces as it cooks.

- Once the meat is fully done add in: the basil, spinach, parsley, oregano, and chives.
- Stir the mix and cook everything for 60 more secs then shut the heat.
- Get a bowl, combine: parmesan, egg whites, feta, and ricotta. Stir the mix then add in the black pepper and turkey mix.
- On a working surface place a large piece of wax paper and lay out the pasta.
- Form your cheese mix into eight balls and put one ball on each piece of lasagna and roll everything up into a burrito shape.
- Continue this process with all of your noodles.
- Now coat the bottom of a casserole dish with tomato sauce and then layer your lasagna rolls over the sauce with seam portion facing downwards in the sauce.
- Top the rolls with the rest of the pasta sauce and a layering of cheddar.
- Place a covering of foil around the dish and put everything in oven for 45 mins.
- Enjoy.

Amount per serving (4 total)

Timing Information:

| Preparation | 40 m |
|---|---|
| Cooking | 1 h |
| Total Time | 1 h 40 m |

Nutritional Information:

| Calories | 637 kcal |
|---|---|
| Fat | 21.6 g |
| Carbohydrates | 70.1g |
| Protein | 44.3 g |
| Cholesterol | 87 mg |
| Sodium | 1281 mg |

* Percent Daily Values are based on a 2,000 calorie diet.

# ITALIAN STYLE RICE

## Ingredients

- 1 C. uncooked white rice
- 2 C. water
- 2 tsps olive oil
- 3 cloves garlic, finely diced
- 1/2 lb lean ground beef
- salt and pepper to taste
- 1/2 C. tomato-based pasta sauce
- 1/2 C. grated Parmesan cheese
- 1/2 C. shredded mozzarella cheese
- 2 eggs, beaten
- 1 C. dry bread crumbs
- 1 1/2 C. tomato-based pasta sauce

## Directions

- Get your rice boiling in water, set the heat to low, place a lid on the pot, and let the rice cook for 22 mins.
- Now begin to stir fry your garlic in olive oil for 5 mins then add in the beef.
- Continue to fry the meat until it is fully done for 12 mins then remove any excess oils.
- Get a bowl, combine: 1/2 C. pasta sauce, rice, pepper, beef, and salt.
- Stir the mix then add in the mozzarella and parmesan.

- Let the cheese melt, then using your hands, shape the mix into balls of about 2 inches.
- Lay all the rice balls onto a cookie sheet.
- Now set your oven to 350 degrees before doing anything else.
- Place the rice balls into the fridge for 30 mins. Then coat the balls with whisked eggs and bread crumbs.
- Place them back on the sheet and cook everything in the oven for 30 mins.
- Now get 2.5 C. of tomato sauce hot while the rice balls cook and when they are done coat everything with the hot tomato sauce.
- Enjoy.

Amount per serving (4 total)

Timing Information:

| Preparation | 15 m |
|---|---|
| Cooking | 45 m |
| Total Time | 1 h 20 m |

Nutritional Information:

| Calories | 643 kcal |
|---|---|
| Fat | 22.1 g |
| Carbohydrates | 77.5g |
| Protein | 30.9 g |
| Cholesterol | 150 mg |
| Sodium | 1025 mg |

* Percent Daily Values are based on a 2,000 calorie diet.

# CHICKEN FROM MILAN

Ingredients

- 1 tbsp butter
- 2 cloves garlic, minced
- 1/2 C. sun-dried tomatoes, diced
- 1 C. chicken broth, divided
- 1 C. heavy cream

- 1 lb skinless, boneless chicken breast halves
- salt and pepper to taste
- 2 tbsps vegetable oil
- 2 tbsps diced fresh basil
- 8 oz. dry fettuccini pasta

Directions

- Stir fry your garlic for 1 min, in butter, then combine in 3/4 C. of broth and the tomatoes.
- Turn up the heat and get everything boiling.
- Once the mix is boiling, set the heat to low, and let the contents cook for 12 mins.
- Now add in the cream and get everything boiling again until the mix is thick.
- Coat your chicken all over with pepper and salt then fry the meat in hot oil for 5 mins each side until fully done. Then place the chicken to the side in a covered bowl.

- Remove some of the drippings from the pan and begin to get 1/4 C. of broth boiling while scraping the bottom bits.
- Once the mix is boiling, set the heat to low, add in the basil, and let the broth reduce a bit.
- Once it has reduced, combine it with the tomato cream sauce.
- Now begin to boil your pasta in water and salt for 9 mins then remove the liquid and place everything in a bowl.
- Stir the pasta with about 5 tbsps of tomato cream sauce.
- Now slice your chicken into strips and get the tomato hot again.
- Divide your noodles between serving dishes.
- Top the noodles with some chicken and then some sauce.
- Enjoy.

Amount per serving (4 total)

Timing Information:

| Preparation | 10 m |
|---|---|
| Cooking | 20 m |
| Total Time | 30 m |

Nutritional Information:

| Calories | 641 kcal |
|---|---|
| Fat | 34.8 g |
| Carbohydrates | 47g |
| Protein | 36.3 g |
| Cholesterol | 156 mg |
| Sodium | 501 mg |

* Percent Daily Values are based on a 2,000 calorie diet.

# CLASSICAL LASAGNA I

## Ingredients

- 1 1/2 lbs lean ground beef
- 1 onion, diced
- 2 cloves garlic, minced
- 1 tbsp diced fresh basil
- 1 tsp dried oregano
- 2 tbsps brown sugar
- 1 1/2 tsps salt
- 1 (29 oz.) can diced tomatoes
- 2 (6 oz.) cans tomato paste
- 12 dry lasagna noodles

- 2 eggs, beaten
- 1 pint part-skim ricotta cheese
- 1/2 C. grated Parmesan cheese
- 2 tbsps dried parsley
- 1 tsp salt
- 1 lb mozzarella cheese, shredded
- 2 tbsps grated Parmesan cheese

## Directions

- Stir fry your garlic, onions, and beef for 3 mins then combine in: tomato paste, basil, diced tomatoes, oregano, 1.5 tsp salt, and brown sugar.
- Now set your oven to 375 degrees before doing anything else.
- Begin to boil your pasta in water and salt for 9 mins then remove all the liquids.

- Get a bowl, combine: 1 tsp salt, eggs, parsley, ricotta, and parmesan.
- Place a third of the pasta in a casserole dish and top everything with half of the cheese mix, one third of the sauce, and 1/2 of the mozzarella.
- Continue layering in this manner until all the ingredients have been used up.
- Then top everything with some more parmesan.
- Cook the lasagna in the oven for 35 mins.
- Enjoy.

Amount per serving (8 total)

Timing Information:

| Preparation | 30 m |
|---|---|
| Cooking | 1 h 30 m |
| Total Time | 2 h |

Nutritional Information:

| Calories | 664 kcal |
|---|---|
| Fat | 29.5 g |
| Carbohydrates | 48.3g |
| Protein | 50.9 g |
| Cholesterol | 1168 mg |
| Sodium | 1900 mg |

* Percent Daily Values are based on a 2,000 calorie diet.

# CLASSICAL LASAGNA II

## Ingredients

- 1 lb sweet Italian sausage
- 3/4 lb lean ground beef
- 1/2 C. minced onion
- 2 cloves garlic, crushed
- 1 (28 oz.) can crushed tomatoes
- 2 (6 oz.) cans tomato paste
- 2 (6.5 oz.) cans canned tomato sauce
- 1/2 C. water
- 2 tbsps white sugar
- 1 1/2 tsps dried basil leaves
- 1/2 tsp fennel seeds

- 1 tsp Italian seasoning
- 1 tbsp salt
- 1/4 tsp ground black pepper
- 4 tbsps diced fresh parsley
- 12 lasagna noodles
- 16 oz. ricotta cheese
- 1 egg
- 1/2 tsp salt
- 3/4 lb mozzarella cheese, sliced
- 3/4 C. grated Parmesan cheese

## Directions

- Stir fry your garlic, sausage, onion, and beef until the meat is fully done. Then add in: 2 tbsp parsley, crushed tomatoes, pepper, tomato paste, 1 tbsp salt, tomato sauce, Italian spice, water, fennel seeds, sugar, and basil.

- Get the mix boiling, set the heat to low, and let the contents gently cook for 90 mins. Stir the mix at least 4 times.
- Now get your pasta boiling in water and salt for 9 mins then remove the liquids.
- Get a bowl, combine: 1/2 tsp salt, ricotta, the rest of the parsley, and the eggs.
- Set your oven to 375 degrees before doing anything else.
- Coat the bottom of a casserole dish with 1.5 C. of the meat and tomato mix then place six pieces of lasagna on top.
- Add half of the cheese mix then 1/3 of the mozzarella.
- Add 1.5 C. of tomato meat mix again and a quarter of a C. of parmesan.
- Continue layering in this manner until all the ingredients have been used up.
- Try to end with mozzarella and parmesan.
- Take a large piece of foil and coat it with nonstick spray then cover the casserole dish with the foil and cook everything in the oven for 30 mins.
- Now take off the foil and continue cooking the lasagna for 20 more mins.
- Serve the dish after letting everything rest for at least 30 mins (longer is better).
- Enjoy.

Amount per serving (12 total)

Timing Information:

| Preparation | 30 m |
|---|---|
| Cooking | 2 h 30 m |
| Total Time | 3 h 15 m |

Nutritional Information:

| Calories | 448 kcal |
|---|---|
| Fat | 21.3 g |
| Carbohydrates | 36.5g |
| Protein | 29.7 g |
| Cholesterol | 82 mg |
| Sodium | 1788 mg |

* Percent Daily Values are based on a 2,000 calorie diet.

# CLAMS, SHRIMP, AND SNAPPER STEW

Ingredients

- 1 tbsp olive oil
- 1 onion, diced
- 3 cloves garlic, finely diced
- 1 carrot, diced
- 2 celery ribs, diced
- 2 bay leaves
- 1 C. diced fresh parsley
- red pepper flakes to taste
- 1 (28 oz.) can whole peeled tomatoes, mashed
- 1 1/2 lbs red snapper fillets, cut into 2 inch pieces
- 1/2 C. white vinegar
- salt and ground black pepper to taste
- 3 C. fish stock
- 1 lb clams in shell, scrubbed
- 1/2 lb medium shrimp, with shells
- 6 (3/4 inch thick) slices Italian bread, toasted

Directions

- Stir fry the following in olive oil for 7 mins: pepper flakes, onions, parsley, garlic, bay leaves, carrots, celery.
- Now combine in the mashed tomatoes and continue cooking everything for 20 mins then add: wine, vinegar, and fish.

- Let the mix continue to cook for 12 mins then add the stock, set the heat to low, place a lid on the pot, and continue cooking everything for 12 more mins.
- Now slowly add in the clams.
- Let the clams cook for 4 mins until they open then add the shrimp and cook them for 4 more mins as well.
- To serve the dish add a piece of bread to the bottom of a serving bowl and top the bread with the tomato mix.
- Enjoy.

Amount per serving (6 total)

Timing Information:

| Preparation | 10 m |
| Cooking | 1 h |
| Total Time | 1 h 10 m |

Nutritional Information:

| Calories | 395 kcal |
| Fat | 7.4 g |
| Carbohydrates | 31.9g |
| Protein | 48.3 g |
| Cholesterol | 125 mg |
| Sodium | 1006 mg |

* Percent Daily Values are based on a 2,000 calorie diet.

# Meatballs Done Right

Ingredients

- 3 lbs lean ground beef
- 5 tbsps ground oregano
- 5 tbsps dried parsley, crushed
- 1 clove garlic, diced
- 1 (1 oz.) package dry onion soup mix
- 2 C. Italian-style dry bread crumbs
- 3 (28 oz.) jars spaghetti sauce

Directions

- Coat a jelly roll pan with oil then set your oven to 350 degrees before doing anything else.
- Get a bowl, combine: garlic, beef, parsley, and oregano.
- Stir the mix then add in the bread crumbs and the onion soup mix.
- Combine everything evenly then use a 1 oz. scoop to form meatballs from the mix.
- Place the meatballs in the dish and cook them for 65 mins in the oven.
- Once the meatballs are done cooking get your pasta sauce and meatballs boiling in a saucepan.
- Once the mix is boiling set the heat to low and let everything gently cook for 5 hrs. Enjoy.

Amount per serving (8 total)

Timing Information:

| Preparation | 1 h 15 m |
|---|---|
| Cooking | 5 h |
| Total Time | 6 h 15 m |

Nutritional Information:

| Calories | 841 kcal |
|---|---|
| Fat | 45.1 g |
| Carbohydrates | 65.6g |
| Protein | 40.3 g |
| Cholesterol | 134 mg |
| Sodium | 2164 mg |

* Percent Daily Values are based on a 2,000 calorie diet.

# BALSAMIC HAM

Ingredients

- 1 (7 oz.) bag arugula
- 7 oz. Parma ham, torn into thin strips
- 1/4 C. olive oil
- 1/4 C. balsamic vinegar

Directions

- Lay out the arugula on a dish for serving. Then layer your piece of ham on top.
- Coat everything with the balsamic and olive oil.
- Enjoy.

Amount per serving (2 total)

Timing Information:

| Preparation | |
|---|---|
| Cooking | 5 m |
| Total Time | 5 m |

Nutritional Information:

| Calories | 495 kcal |
|---|---|
| Fat | 40.1 g |
| Carbohydrates | 8.3g |
| Protein | 29.2 g |
| Cholesterol | 88 mg |
| Sodium | 1944 mg |

* Percent Daily Values are based on a 2,000 calorie diet.

# CLASSICAL SAUSAGE AND PEPPERS FROM ITALY

Ingredients

- 6 (4 oz.) links sweet Italian sausage
- 2 tbsps butter
- 1 yellow onion, sliced
- 1/2 red onion, sliced
- 4 cloves garlic, minced
- 1 large red bell pepper, sliced
- 1 green bell pepper, sliced
- 1 tsp dried basil
- 1 tsp dried oregano
- 1/4 C. white wine

Directions

- Stir fry your sausage until it is fully browned then place the meat to side and cut it into pieces.
- Now begin to stir fry the following for 5 mins, in butter, in the same pan: garlic, red onions, and yellow onions.
- Now add in the bell peppers, white wine, oregano, and basil.
- Let the mix continue to cook until the onions are soft.
- Add the sausage back to the mix, set the heat to low, place a lid on the pan, and let the contents cook for 20 mins.
- Enjoy.

Amount per serving (6 total)

Timing Information:

| Preparation | 15 m |
|---|---|
| Cooking | 25 m |
| Total Time | 40 m |

Nutritional Information:

| Calories | 461 kcal |
|---|---|
| Fat | 39.4 g |
| Carbohydrates | 7g |
| Protein | 17.1 g |
| Cholesterol | 96 mg |
| Sodium | 857 mg |

* Percent Daily Values are based on a 2,000 calorie diet.

# Easy Biscotti

## Ingredients

- 3/4 C. butter
- 1 C. white sugar
- 2 eggs
- 1 1/2 tsps vanilla extract
- 2 1/2 C. all-purpose flour
- 1 tsp ground cinnamon
- 3/4 tsp baking powder
- 1/2 tsp salt
- 1 C. hazelnuts

## Directions

- Coat a baking dish with oil then set your oven to 350 degrees before doing anything else.
- Get a bowl, combine: sugar and butter. Mix the contents until it is creamy.
- Now add in the vanilla and the eggs. Stir the mix then sift in: salt, flour, baking powder, and cinnamon. Stir everything again then add in the hazelnuts.
- Now form your dough into 2 foot long cylinders.
- Lay the cylinders on the cookie sheet and flatten them.
- Let the dough cook in the oven for 35 mins. Then let the loaves lose their heat.

- Now cut each one diagonally and place everything back in the oven for 12 more mins.
- Flip the loaves after 6 mins of cooking.
- Enjoy.

Amount per serving (30 total)

Timing Information:

| | |
|---|---|
| Preparation | 25 m |
| Cooking | 40 m |
| Total Time | 1 h 35 m |

Nutritional Information:

| | |
|---|---|
| Calories | 138 kcal |
| Fat | 7.8 g |
| Carbohydrates | 15.5g |
| Protein | 2.2 g |
| Cholesterol | 25 mg |
| Sodium | 89 mg |

* Percent Daily Values are based on a 2,000 calorie diet.

# Italian Tuscan Soup

Ingredients

- 1 (16 oz.) package smoked sausage
- 2 potatoes, cut into 1/4-inch slices
- 3/4 C. diced onion
- 6 slices bacon
- 1 1/2 tsps minced garlic
- 2 C. kale - washed, dried, and shredded
- 2 tbsps chicken bouillon powder
- 1 quart water
- 1/3 C. heavy whipping cream

Directions

- Set your oven to 300 degrees before doing anything else.
- Place your pieces of sausage on a cookie sheet and cook everything in the oven for 30 mins. Then divide the meat in half and then cut them in half again diagonally. Begin to stir fry your bacon and onions until the onions are translucent then remove the bacon from the pan.
- Add in the garlic and cook everything for 2 more mins then add the chicken base, potatoes, and water.
- Let the mix gently boil for 20 mins then add in: the cream, bacon, kale, and sausage.
- Let the soup cook for 5 mins. Enjoy.

Amount per serving (6 total)

Timing Information:

| Preparation | 15 m |
|---|---|
| Cooking | 55 m |
| Total Time | 1 h 10 m |

Nutritional Information:

| Calories | 459 kcal |
|---|---|
| Fat | 34.1 g |
| Carbohydrates | 21.1g |
| Protein | 17.2 g |
| Cholesterol | 87 mg |
| Sodium | 1925 mg |

* Percent Daily Values are based on a 2,000 calorie diet.

# CHICKEN MARSALA CLASSICO

Ingredients

- 1/4 C. all-purpose flour for coating
- 1/2 tsp salt
- 1/4 tsp ground black pepper
- 1/2 tsp dried oregano
- 4 skinless, boneless chicken breast halves – flattened to 1/4 inch thick

- 4 tbsps butter
- 4 tbsps olive oil
- 1 C. sliced mushrooms
- 1/2 C. Marsala wine
- 1/4 C. cooking sherry

Directions

- Get a bowl, combine: oregano, flour, pepper, and salt.
- Dredge your pieces of chicken in the mix then begin to stir fry the chicken in butter.
- Let the chicken fry until it is browned all over then add in: the sherry, mushrooms, and wine.
- Place a lid on the pan and let the contents gently boil for 12 mins.
- Enjoy.

Amount per serving (4 total)

Timing Information:

| Preparation | 10 m |
|---|---|
| Cooking | 20 m |
| Total Time | 30 m |

Nutritional Information:

| Calories | 448 kcal |
|---|---|
| Fat | 26.6 g |
| Carbohydrates | 13.3g |
| Protein | 28.8 g |
| Cholesterol | 99 mg |
| Sodium | 543 mg |

* Percent Daily Values are based on a 2,000 calorie diet.

# Maggie's Easy Bruschetta

Ingredients

- 6 roma (plum) tomatoes, diced
- 1/2 C. sun-dried tomatoes, packed in oil
- 3 cloves minced garlic
- 1/4 C. olive oil
- 2 tbsps balsamic vinegar
- 1/4 C. fresh basil, stems removed
- 1/4 tsp salt
- 1/4 tsp ground black pepper
- 1 French baguette
- 2 C. shredded mozzarella cheese

Directions

- Get your oven's broiler hot before doing anything else.
- Now grab a bowl, mix: pepper, roma tomatoes, salt, sun-dried tomatoes, basil, garlic, vinegar, and olive oil. Let this mix sit for 12 mins and begin to slice your bread into 3/4 of inch pieces.
- Place the pieces of bread on a cookie sheet then place everything under the broiler for 3 mins.
- Now evenly top each piece of bread with the roma tomato mix.
- Then add a piece of cheese on top of each one.
- Cook the bread slices under the broiler for 6 more mins. Enjoy.

Amount per serving (12 total)

Timing Information:

| Preparation | 15 m |
|---|---|
| Cooking | 7 m |
| Total Time | 35 m |

Nutritional Information:

| Calories | 215 kcal |
|---|---|
| Fat | 8.9 g |
| Carbohydrates | 24.8g |
| Protein | 9.6 g |
| Cholesterol | 12 mg |
| Sodium | 426 mg |

* Percent Daily Values are based on a 2,000 calorie diet.

# Authentic Eggplant Parmesan

Ingredients

- 3 eggplant, peeled and thinly sliced
- 2 eggs, beaten
- 4 C. Italian seasoned bread crumbs
- 6 C. spaghetti sauce, divided
- 1 (16 oz.) package mozzarella cheese, shredded and divided
- 1/2 C. grated Parmesan cheese, divided
- 1/2 tsp dried basil

Directions

- Set your oven to 350 degrees before doing anything else.
- Coat your pieces of eggplant with egg then with bread crumbs.
- Now lay the veggies on a cookie sheet and cook them in the oven for 6 mins. Flip the eggplants and cook them for 6 more mins.
- Coat the bottom of a casserole dish with pasta sauce then layer some of your eggplants in the dish.
- Top the veggies with some parmesan and mozzarella then layer your eggplants, sauce, and cheese.
- Continue this pattern until all the ingredients have been used up.
- Finally coat the layer with some basil and cook everything in the oven for 40 mins. Enjoy.

Amount per serving (10 total)

Timing Information:

| Preparation | 25 m |
|---|---|
| Cooking | 35 m |
| Total Time | 1 h |

Nutritional Information:

| Calories | 487 kcal |
|---|---|
| Fat | 16 g |
| Carbohydrates | 62.1g |
| Protein | 24.2 g |
| Cholesterol | 73 mg |
| Sodium | 1663 mg |

* Percent Daily Values are based on a 2,000 calorie diet.

# ROMAN FUN PASTA

## Ingredients

- 1 (12 oz.) package bow tie pasta
- 2 tbsps olive oil
- 1 lb sweet Italian sausage, casings removed and crumbled
- 1/2 tsp red pepper flakes
- 1/2 C. diced onion
- 3 cloves garlic, minced
- 1 (28 oz.) can Italian-style plum tomatoes, drained and coarsely diced
- 1 1/2 C. heavy cream
- 1/2 tsp salt
- 3 tbsps minced fresh parsley

## Directions

- Boil your pasta in water and salt for 9 mins then remove the liquids.
- Begin to stir fry your pepper flakes and sausage in oil until it the meat is browned then add the garlic and onions. Let the onions cook until they are soft then add in the salt, cream, and tomatoes.
- Stir the mix then get everything gently boiling.
- Let the mix gently cook with a low level of heat for 9 mins then add in the pasta.
- Stir the mix, to evenly cook the noodles, then coat everything with parsley. Enjoy.

Amount per serving (6 total)

Timing Information:

| Preparation | 15 m |
|---|---|
| Cooking | 30 m |
| Total Time | 45 m |

Nutritional Information:

| Calories | 656 kcal |
|---|---|
| Fat | 42.1 g |
| Carbohydrates | 50.9g |
| Protein | 20.1 g |
| Cholesterol | 111 mg |
| Sodium | 1088 mg |

* Percent Daily Values are based on a 2,000 calorie diet.

# Zucchini and Spinach Soup

## Ingredients

- 1 lb Italian sausage
- 1 clove garlic, minced
- 2 (14 oz.) cans beef broth
- 1 (14.5 oz.) can Italian-style stewed tomatoes
- 1 C. sliced carrots
- 1 (14.5 oz.) can great Northern beans, undrained
- 2 small zucchini, cubed
- 2 C. spinach - packed, rinsed and torn
- 1/4 tsp ground black pepper
- 1/4 tsp salt

## Directions

- Stir fry your garlic and sausage, in a large pot, for 2 mins then combine in the pepper, broth, salt, tomato, and carrots.
- Stir the mix, place a lid on the pot, and let everything gently boil for 20 mins with a medium to low level of heat.
- Now add in the zucchini and beans with their sauce.
- Place the lid back on the pot and continue cooking everything for 17 more mins.
- Now shut the heat, stir in the spinach, and place the lid back on the pot.
- Let the spinach wilt for 7 mins then serve the soup. Enjoy.

Amount per serving (6 total)

Timing Information:

| Preparation | 10 m |
|---|---|
| Cooking | 40 m |
| Total Time | 50 m |

Nutritional Information:

| Calories | 385 kcal |
|---|---|
| Fat | 24.4 g |
| Carbohydrates | 22.5g |
| Protein | 18.8 g |
| Cholesterol | 58 mg |
| Sodium | 1259 mg |

* Percent Daily Values are based on a 2,000 calorie diet.

# Italian Rump Roast

Ingredients

- 3 C. water
- 1 tsp salt
- 1 tsp ground black pepper
- 1 tsp dried oregano
- 1 tsp dried basil
- 1 tsp onion salt
- 1 tsp dried parsley
- 1 tsp garlic powder
- 1 bay leaf
- 1 (.7 oz.) package dry Italian-style salad dressing mix
- 1 (5 lb) rump roast

Directions

- Get the following boiling in a large pot: salad dressing mix, water, salt, bay leaf, black pepper, garlic, oregano, parsley, basil, and onion salt.
- Once the mix is boiling add the roast to the crock of a slow cooker and top the mix with the simmering liquid.
- Place the lid on the slow cooker and let everything cook for 11 hrs with low heat.
- Now remove the meat and shred it into pieces.
- Place the shredded meat back into the crock pot and let it cook for 20 more mins with a low level of heat.
- Enjoy.

Amount per serving (10 total)

Timing Information:

| Preparation | 15 m |
|---|---|
| Cooking | 12 h |
| Total Time | 12 h 15 m |

Nutritional Information:

| Calories | 318 kcal |
|---|---|
| Fat | 15.8 g |
| Carbohydrates | 1.6g |
| Protein | 39.4 g |
| Cholesterol | 100 mg |
| Sodium | 819 mg |

* Percent Daily Values are based on a 2,000 calorie diet.

# CLASSICAL RISOTTO

## Ingredients

- 6 C. chicken broth, divided
- 3 tbsps olive oil, divided
- 1 lb portobello mushrooms, thinly sliced
- 1 lb white mushrooms, thinly sliced
- 2 shallots, diced
- 1 1/2 C. Arborio rice
- 1/2 C. dry white wine
- sea salt to taste
- freshly ground black pepper to taste
- 3 tbsps finely diced chives
- 4 tbsps butter
- 1/3 C. freshly grated Parmesan cheese

## Directions

- Get your broth warm with a low level of heat. Then begin to stir fry your mushrooms in 2 tbsp of olive oil for 4 mins.
- Now remove everything from the pot and add in 1 more tbsp of olive oil and begin to fry your shallots in it for 2 mins then add in the rice and stir fry it for 3 mins.
- Pour in the wine while continuing to stir, and keep stirring, until it is absorbed.

- Once the wine has been absorbed combine in half a C. of broth and keep stirring until it is absorbed as well.
- Now for about 20 mins keep pouring in half a C. of broth and stirring the mix until the broth is absorbed by the rice.
- After 20 mins of forming the risotto, shut the heat and combine in: the parmesan, pepper, mushrooms and their juice, chives, salt, and butter.
- Enjoy.

Amount per serving (6 total)

Timing Information:

| Preparation | 20 m |
|---|---|
| Cooking | 30 m |
| Total Time | 50 m |

Nutritional Information:

| Calories | 431 kcal |
|---|---|
| Fat | 16.6 g |
| Carbohydrates | 56.6g |
| Protein | 11.3 g |
| Cholesterol | 29 mg |
| Sodium | 1131 mg |

* Percent Daily Values are based on a 2,000 calorie diet.

# TORTELLINI CLASSICO

## Ingredients

- 1 lb sweet Italian sausage, casings removed
- 1 C. diced onion
- 2 cloves garlic, minced
- 5 C. beef broth
- 1/2 C. water
- 1/2 C. red wine
- 4 large tomatoes - peeled, seeded and diced
- 1 C. thinly sliced carrots
- 1/2 tbsp packed fresh basil leaves
- 1/2 tsp dried oregano
- 1 (8 oz.) can tomato sauce
- 1 1/2 C. sliced zucchini
- 8 oz. fresh tortellini pasta
- 3 tbsps diced fresh parsley

## Directions

- In a large pot brown your sausage all over.
- Then remove the meat from the pan.
- Begin to stir fry your garlic and onions in the drippings then add in: the sausage, broth, tomato sauce, water, oregano, wine, basil, tomatoes, and carrots.
- Get the mix boiling, set the heat to low, and let everything cook for 35 mins.

- Remove any fat which rises to the top then add in the parsley and zucchini.
- Continue cooking the mix for 20 more mins before adding in the pasta and letting everything cooking 15 more mins.
- When serving the dish top it with parmesan.
- Enjoy.

Amount per serving (8 total)

Timing Information:

| Preparation | 20 m |
|---|---|
| Cooking | 1 h 15 m |
| Total Time | 1 h 35 m |

Nutritional Information:

| Calories | 324 kcal |
|---|---|
| Fat | 20.2 g |
| Carbohydrates | 19.1g |
| Protein | 14.6 g |
| Cholesterol | 50 mg |
| Sodium | 1145 mg |

* Percent Daily Values are based on a 2,000 calorie diet.

# FETA FETTUCINE

Ingredients

- 1 bunch diced fresh cilantro
- 6 tbsps pine nuts
- 1 tsp lemon juice, or to taste
- 1/3 C. crumbled feta cheese
- salt and ground black pepper to taste
- 1/2 C. olive oil
- 1 (12 oz.) package fettucine pasta
- 1 tsp extra-virgin olive oil

Directions

- Pulse the following in a food processor until minced: black pepper, cilantro, salt, pine nuts, feta cheese, and lemon juice.
- Now slowly add in half a C. of olive oil while continually running the processor.
- Boil your pasta for 9 mins in water and salt then remove the liquids.
- Place the pasta in a bowl and top it with the cilantro sauce.
- Toss the mix then add some olive oil and toss everything again.
- Enjoy.

Amount per serving (4 total)

Timing Information:

| Preparation | 15 m |
|---|---|
| Cooking | 10 m |
| Total Time | 25 m |

Nutritional Information:

| Calories | 663 kcal |
|---|---|
| Fat | 39.4 g |
| Carbohydrates | 64.8g |
| Protein | 16.5 g |
| Cholesterol | 11 mg |
| Sodium | 248 mg |

* Percent Daily Values are based on a 2,000 calorie diet.

# AUTHENTIC MEATBALL SUB

## Ingredients

- 1 1/2 lbs lean ground beef
- 1/3 C. Italian seasoned bread crumbs
- 1/2 small onion, diced
- 1 tsp salt
- 1/2 C. shredded mozzarella cheese, divided
- 1 tbsp cracked black pepper
- 1 tsp garlic powder
- 1/2 C. marinara sauce
- 3 hoagie rolls, split lengthwise

## Directions

- Set your oven to 350 degrees before doing anything else.
- Get a bowl, combine: 1/2 of the mozzarella, beef, garlic powder, bread crumbs, pepper, onions, and salt. Shape the mix into a large loaf then place it in a casserole dish. Cook the meat in the oven for 55 mins then let it cool for 10 mins.
- Cut the meat into slices then layer the pieces of meat on a roll.
- Top everything with the marinara then add a topping of cheese.
- Cover the sandwich with some foil and put everything in the oven for 20 more mins.
- Let the sandwich cool for 20 mins then cut each one in half. Enjoy.

Amount per serving (6 total)

Timing Information:

| Preparation | 15 m |
|---|---|
| Cooking | 1 h 5 m |
| Total Time | 1 h 40 m |

Nutritional Information:

| Calories | 491 kcal |
|---|---|
| Fat | 21.4 g |
| Carbohydrates | 43.1g |
| Protein | 29.3 g |
| Cholesterol | 75 mg |
| Sodium | 1068 mg |

* Percent Daily Values are based on a 2,000 calorie diet.

# ATHENIAN PORK LOINS

## Ingredients

- 1 tsp olive oil
- 2 C. sliced mushrooms
- 2 tbsps olive oil
- 6 (3/4 inch thick) pork loin chops
- 2 cloves garlic, crushed
- 1 C. diced onion
- 1 (14.5 oz.) can diced Italian tomatoes, undrained
- 1 tsp dried basil
- 1/2 tsp dried oregano
- 1/2 tsp salt
- 1/4 tsp ground black pepper
- 1/2 C. water, if necessary
- 1 large green bell pepper, cut in 6 pieces

## Directions

- Stir fry your mushrooms in 1 tsp of olive oil for 9 mins then place the veggies in a bowl.
- Add the rest of the olive oil to the pan and begin to fry your pork for 9 mins until browned all over.
- Remove the pork from the pan as well and remove most of the drippings but keep about 2 tbsps of it.
- Begin to stir fry your onion and garlic in the drippings for 7 mins then add in: the pepper, tomatoes, salt, oregano, and basil.

- Stir the mix then add your pork to the pot as well.
- Continue cooking everything for 50 mins. Then add some water if needed.
- Now add the bell peppers on top of everything and the mushrooms as well.
- Let the mix keep cooking for 7 more mins.
- Enjoy.

Amount per serving (6 total)

Timing Information:

| Preparation | 15 m |
|---|---|
| Cooking | 1 h 10 m |
| Total Time | 1 h 25 m |

Nutritional Information:

| Calories | 290 kcal |
|---|---|
| Fat | 17.6 g |
| Carbohydrates | 7.8g |
| Protein | 25.4 g |
| Cholesterol | 63 mg |
| Sodium | 339 mg |

* Percent Daily Values are based on a 2,000 calorie diet.

# CAPERS AND TILAPIA

Ingredients

- 2 tbsps extra virgin olive oil
- 2 tbsps butter
- 1 tbsp minced garlic
- 1 lb tilapia fillets
- salt and ground black pepper to taste
- 1/2 C. sliced fresh button mushrooms
- 2 tbsps drained capers
- 1/2 C. white wine
- 1 lemon, juiced

Directions

- Stir fry your garlic in butter and olive oil then add the pieces of fish to pan.
- Top the fish with pepper and salt and fry everything for 3 mins. Flip the fish then coat the opposite side with pepper and salt as well and fry it for 3 mins.
- Now combine in the wine, capers, and mushrooms.
- Place a lid on the pot, set the heat to low, and simmer the mix for 8 mins.
- Take off the lid, add in the lemon juice, and continue cooking everything for 2 more mins.
- Enjoy.

Amount per serving (4 total)

Timing Information:

| Preparation | 15 m |
|---|---|
| Cooking | 10 m |
| Total Time | 25 m |

Nutritional Information:

| Calories | 262 kcal |
|---|---|
| Fat | 14.2 g |
| Carbohydrates | 5g |
| Protein | 24.2 g |
| Cholesterol | 57 mg |
| Sodium | 222 mg |

* Percent Daily Values are based on a 2,000 calorie diet.

# Southern Italian Chicken

## Ingredients

- 3 cloves garlic, minced
- 1/3 C. pitted prunes, halved
- 8 small green olives
- 2 tbsps capers, with liquid
- 2 tbsps olive oil
- 2 tbsps red wine vinegar
- 2 bay leaves
- 1 tbsp dried oregano
- salt and pepper to taste
- 1 (3 lb) whole chicken, skin removed and cut into pieces
- 1/4 C. packed brown sugar
- 1/4 C. dry white wine
- 1 tbsp diced fresh parsley, for garnish

## Directions

- Get a bowl, combine: pepper, garlic, salt, prunes, oregano, olives, bay leaves, capers, vinegar, and olive oil.
- Layer this mix in the bottom of casserole dish then layer the chicken on top. Stir everything then place a covering of plastic around the dish.
- Put everything in the fridge for 8 hrs.
- Now set your oven to 350 degrees before doing anything else.
- Once the oven is hot pour the wine and the brown sugar around the chicken and begin to cook everything in the oven for 65 mins.

- Baste the meat with the surrounding sauce at least 5 times.
- When serving the dish top everything with the sauce and drippings and also some fresh parsley.
- Enjoy.

Amount per serving (6 total)

Timing Information:

| Preparation | 15 m |
| Cooking | 1 h |
| Total Time | 9 h 15 m |

Nutritional Information:

| Calories | 402 kcal |
| Fat | 22.4 g |
| Carbohydrates | 16.5g |
| Protein | 31.2 g |
| Cholesterol | 97 mg |
| Sodium | 308 mg |

* Percent Daily Values are based on a 2,000 calorie diet.

# ROAST BEEF SANDWICHES

Ingredients

- 3 lbs beef chuck roast
- 3 (1 oz.) packages dry Italian salad dressing mix
- 1 C. water
- 1 (16 oz.) jar pepperoncini peppers
- 8 hamburger buns, split

Directions

- Place your chuck in the crock of a slow cooker and top the meat with the dressing mix.
- Now add the water and place a lid on the slow cooker.
- Cook the meat for 6 hrs with a high level of heat.
- At the fifth hour remove the meat and shred it into pieces.
- The meat should easily shred if not add it back to the crock pot.
- After shredding the meat combine in the peppers and some of the juice.
- Enjoy with the buns.

Amount per serving (6 total)

Timing Information:

| Preparation | 10 m |
|---|---|
| Cooking | 6 h |
| Total Time | 6 h 10 m |

Nutritional Information:

| Calories | 557 kcal |
|---|---|
| Fat | 28.8 g |
| Carbohydrates | 38.4g |
| Protein | 31.9 g |
| Cholesterol | 103 mg |
| Sodium | 4233 mg |

* Percent Daily Values are based on a 2,000 calorie diet.

# Mediterranean Pork

Ingredients

- 2 tbsps steak seasoning rub
- 1/2 C. balsamic vinegar
- 1/2 C. olive oil
- 2 lbs boneless pork loin roast

Directions

- Get a bowl, combine: olive oil, balsamic, and steak seasoning.
- Stir the mix until it is smooth then add in the pork and stir everything again.
- Place a covering of plastic on the bowl and put everything in the fridge for 5 hrs.
- Now set your oven to 350 degrees before doing anything else.
- Lay out your pieces of meat in a casserole dish and top the meat with the marinade.
- Cook everything in the oven for 65 mins then baste the meat at least 4 times.
- Carve the meat then serve it.
- Enjoy.

Amount per serving (8 total)

Timing Information:

| Preparation | 5 m |
|-------------|-----|
| Cooking | 1 h |
| Total Time | 3 h 5 m |

Nutritional Information:

| Calories | 299 kcal |
|----------|----------|
| Fat | 23.4 g |
| Carbohydrates | 3.1g |
| Protein | 18.3 g |
| Cholesterol | 55 mg |
| Sodium | 732 mg |

* Percent Daily Values are based on a 2,000 calorie diet.

# TORTELLINI

Ingredients

- 1 (16 oz.) package cheese tortellini
- 1 (14.5 oz.) can diced tomatoes with garlic and onion
- 1 C. diced fresh spinach
- 1/2 tsp salt
- 1/4 tsp pepper
- 1 1/2 tsps dried basil
- 1 tsp minced garlic
- 2 tbsps all-purpose flour
- 3/4 C. milk
- 3/4 C. heavy cream
- 1/4 C. grated Parmesan cheese

Directions

- Boil your pasta in water and salt for 9 mins then remove the liquids.
- At the same time heat and stir the following in a large pot: garlic, tomatoes, basil, spinach, pepper and salt.
- Once the mix begins to simmer add in a mix of cream, milk, and flour.
- Stir the mix until everything is smooth then add the parmesan and set the heat to low.
- Let the mix gently boil for 4 mins then add in your pasta to the sauce after it has cooked.
- Stir everything. Enjoy.

Amount per serving (6 total)

Timing Information:

| Preparation | 20 m |
|---|---|
| Cooking | 20 m |
| Total Time | 40 m |

Nutritional Information:

| Calories | 400 kcal |
|---|---|
| Fat | 19.7 g |
| Carbohydrates | 43.9g |
| Protein | 14.8 g |
| Cholesterol | 79 mg |
| Sodium | 885 mg |

* Percent Daily Values are based on a 2,000 calorie diet.

# Italian Baked Turkey-Loaf

Ingredients

- cooking spray
- 1 lb ground turkey
- 1 egg
- 1/4 C. Italian seasoned bread crumbs
- 1 tsp Italian seasoning
- 1/2 clove garlic, minced
- 1/2 tsp ground black pepper, or to taste
- 1/4 tsp salt, or to taste
- 2 C. tomato sauce, divided

Directions

- Coat a casserole dish with nonstick spray then set your oven to 400 degrees before doing anything else. Get a bowl, combine: salt, turkey, black pepper, egg, garlic, bread crumbs, and Italian seasoning.
- Form the mix into a loaf and place it in the casserole dish.
- Cook the loaf in the oven for 45 mins then top with 1/2 of the tomato sauce.
- Let the loaf keep cooking for 12 more mins until it is fully done.
- Then leave the meat to sit for 15 mins.
- As the loaf cools get the rest of the tomato sauce hot.
- When serving your loaf top it liberally with the tomato sauce. Enjoy.

Amount per serving (6 total)

Timing Information:

| Preparation | 10 m |
|---|---|
| Cooking | 50 m |
| Total Time | 1 h 5 m |

Nutritional Information:

| Calories | 163 kcal |
|---|---|
| Fat | 7 g |
| Carbohydrates | 8.1g |
| Protein | 17.8 g |
| Cholesterol | 87 mg |
| Sodium | 651 mg |

* Percent Daily Values are based on a 2,000 calorie diet.

# Restaurant Style Primavera

Ingredients

- 1 (16 oz.) package uncooked farfalle pasta
- 1 lb hot Italian turkey sausage, cut into 1/2 inch slices
- 1/2 C. olive oil, divided
- 4 cloves garlic, diced
- 1/2 onion, diced
- 2 small zucchini, diced
- 2 small yellow squash, diced
- 6 roma (plum) tomatoes, diced
- 1 green bell pepper, diced
- 20 leaves fresh basil
- 2 tsps chicken bouillon granules
- 1/2 tsp red pepper flakes
- 1/2 C. grated Parmesan cheese

Directions

- Cook your pasta in water and salt for 9 mins then remove all the liquids.
- Stir fry your sausage until fully done then remove it from the pan.
- Now begin to stir fry your onions and garlic until the mix is hot then add in: basil, zucchini, bell peppers, squash, and tomatoes.
- Stir the mix then add in the bouillon and evenly mix it in.
- Once the bouillon has been added.

- Combine in the red pepper and the rest of the oil.
- Keep cooking the mix for 12 more mins then stir in the cheese, sausage, and pasta.
- Let everything get hot for 7 mins.
- Enjoy.

Amount per serving (8 total)

Timing Information:

| Preparation | 20 m |
|---|---|
| Cooking | 30 m |
| Total Time | 50 m |

Nutritional Information:

| Calories | 477 kcal |
|---|---|
| Fat | 21.8 g |
| Carbohydrates | 50.1g |
| Protein | 20.5 g |
| Cholesterol | 38 mg |
| Sodium | 621 mg |

* Percent Daily Values are based on a 2,000 calorie diet.

# AUTHENTIC ITALIAN TETRAZZINI

## Ingredients

- 2 (8 oz.) packages angel hair pasta
- 1/4 C. butter
- 2/3 C. sliced onion
- 1/4 C. all-purpose flour
- 2 C. milk
- 1 tsp salt
- 1/4 tsp ground white pepper
- 1/2 tsp poultry seasoning
- 1/4 tsp ground mustard
- 1 C. shredded sharp Cheddar cheese, divided
- 2 tbsps diced pimento peppers (optional)
- 1 (4.5 oz.) can sliced mushrooms
- 1 lb cooked turkey, sliced

## Directions

- Set your oven to 400 degrees before doing anything else.
- Boil your pasta in water and salt for 6 mins then remove all the liquids.
- Now begin to stir fry your onions, in butter, until they are soft then add the flour and milk slowly.
- Stir the mix until it is all smooth then add: the mustard, salt, poultry seasoning, and pepper.

- Let the mix heat until it becomes thick. Then continue to stir as the mix cooks.
- Once everything is thick shut the heat and add in your pimento and 2/3 C. of cheese.
- Let the mix cook until the cheese is melted then add in your mushrooms.
- Get a casserole dish and layer your pasta in the bottom of it then place some turkey and cover everything with the cheese sauce.
- Continue laying in this manner until all the ingredients have been used up.
- Now top the layers with the rest of the cheese which should be about 1/3 of a C.
- Cook the contents in the oven for 30 mins.
- Enjoy.

Amount per serving (6 total)

Timing Information:

| Preparation | 25 m |
|---|---|
| Cooking | 25 m |
| Total Time | 50 m |

Nutritional Information:

| Calories | 604 kcal |
|---|---|
| Fat | 26.4 g |
| Carbohydrates | 52.1g |
| Protein | 38.9 g |
| Cholesterol | 113 mg |
| Sodium | 914 mg |

* Percent Daily Values are based on a 2,000 calorie diet.

# Pepperoni, Salami, and Prosciutto Stuffing

Ingredients

- 1 (1 lb) loaf white bread, cut into cubes
- 8 eggs, beaten
- 1 C. diced prosciutto
- 1 C. diced salami
- 4 oz. diced pepperoni
- 16 oz. mozzarella cheese, cubed
- 1/4 C. grated Parmesan cheese
- 2 tbsps diced fresh parsley
- ground black pepper to taste

Directions

- Set your oven to 375 degrees before doing anything else.
- Get a bowl and add in your bread cubes.
- Coat the bread with some water to get everything somewhat moist.
- Now combine in: the pepper, eggs, parsley, prosciutto, parmesan, salami, mozzarella, and pepperoni.
- Add everything to a baking dish and cook it all in the oven for 40 mins.
- Enjoy.

Amount per serving (8 total)

Timing Information:

| Preparation | 10 m |
|---|---|
| Cooking | 50 m |
| Total Time | 1 h |

Nutritional Information:

| Calories | 582 kcal |
|---|---|
| Fat | 33.8 g |
| Carbohydrates | 31.6g |
| Protein | 36.2 g |
| Cholesterol | 273 mg |
| Sodium | 1785 mg |

* Percent Daily Values are based on a 2,000 calorie diet.

# LEMON PESTO FISH

Ingredients

- 2 lbs salmon fillets, de-boned
- 2 lemons
- 1 1/2 C. pesto
- 1/2 C. white wine

Directions

- Coat a baking pan with oil then lay your pieces of fish in it with the skin of the fish facing downwards.
- Coat the fish with the juice of one freshly squeezed lemon then top everything with the wine.
- Let the fish sit in the dish for 20 mins.
- Now get your oven's broiler hot before doing anything else.
- Lay your pesto over the pieces of fish evenly and cook everything under the broiler.
- For every 1 inch of thickness in your fish. Broil it for 9 mins.
- Now take out the fish from the oven and top them with the juice of a 2nd freshly squeezed lemon.
- Cut the rest of the lemon into thin pieces and layer them over the fish.
- Enjoy.

Amount per serving (4 total)

Timing Information:

| Preparation | 10 m |
|---|---|
| Cooking | 15 m |
| Total Time | 40 m |

Nutritional Information:

| Calories | 917 kcal |
|---|---|
| Fat | 67.4 g |
| Carbohydrates | 112.7g |
| Protein | 62.6 g |
| Cholesterol | 1164 mg |
| Sodium | 851 mg |

* Percent Daily Values are based on a 2,000 calorie diet.

# Authentic Calamari

Ingredients

- 12 calamari tubes, cleaned and dried
- 2 green onions, finely diced
- 6 cloves garlic, minced
- 1/2 lb diced cooked shrimp meat
- 1/2 lb cooked crabmeat, diced
- 1 tbsp lemon juice
- 3/4 C. butter
- 12 oz. cream cheese, cut into cubes
- 2 cloves garlic, minced
- 3 C. milk
- 10 oz. freshly grated Parmesan cheese
- 1 pinch ground black pepper
- 3/4 C. freshly grated Romano cheese
- 1 (8 oz.) package linguine pasta

Directions

- Set your oven to 350 degrees before doing anything else.
- Get a bowl, combine: lemon juice, onions, crabmeat, 6 pieces of garlic, and shrimp.
- Divide this mix amongst your tubes of squid then stake the tubes closed with a toothpick.

- Place everything into a casserole dish.
- Begin to heat and stir 2 cloves of garlic and cream cheese in butter until the cheese is melted.
- Slowly add in your milk and keep stirring until all the milk is hot and everything is smooth.
- Now add the pepper and parmesan.
- Top the contents of the casserole dish with this mix. Then add 2 tbsp of Romano over everything.
- Cook the mix in the oven until the cheese has melted and is browned.
- At the same time begin to boil your pasta in water and salt for 9 mins then remove the liquid.
- Serve the calamad over the pasta with a liber amount of sauce.
- Enjoy.

Amount per serving (6 total)

Timing Information:

| Preparation | 20 m |
|---|---|
| Cooking | 20 m |
| Total Time | 40 m |

Nutritional Information:

| Calories | 1019 kcal |
|---|---|
| Fat | 65.6 g |
| Carbohydrates | 141.7g |
| Protein | 65.6 g |
| Cholesterol | 1479 mg |
| Sodium | 11549 mg |

* Percent Daily Values are based on a 2,000 calorie diet.

# Northern California Cioppino

# (Mussel and Clam Italian Stew)

Ingredients

- 3/4 C. butter
- 2 onions, diced
- 2 cloves garlic, minced
- 1 bunch fresh parsley, diced
- 2 (14.5 oz.) cans stewed tomatoes
- 2 (14.5 oz.) cans chicken broth
- 2 bay leaves
- 1 tbsp dried basil
- 1/2 tsp dried thyme
- 1/2 tsp dried oregano
- 1 C. water
- 1 1/2 C. white wine
- 1 1/2 lbs large shrimp - peeled and deveined
- 1 1/2 lbs bay scallops
- 18 small clams
- 18 mussels, cleaned and debearded
- 1 1/2 C. crabmeat
- 1 1/2 lbs cod fillets, cubed

Directions

- Stir fry your parsley, garlic, and onions, in butter, in a large pot.
- Cook the mix until the onions are tender.

- Now combine in the tomatoes, wine, broth, water, bay leaves, thyme, basil, and oregano.
- Place a lid on the pot and let the mix gently boil for 35 mins.
- Now add in the crab, shrimp, mussels, clams, and scallops.
- Stir the mix then add in the fish.
- Get everything boiling then place the lid back on the pot and let the contents cook for 9 more mins until the clams open.
- Divide the mix between bowls then top each with bread.
- Enjoy.

Amount per serving (13 total)

Timing Information:

| Preparation | 10 m |
|---|---|
| Cooking | 45 m |
| Total Time | 55 m |

Nutritional Information:

| Calories | 318 kcal |
|---|---|
| Fat | 12.9 g |
| Carbohydrates | 9.3g |
| Protein | 34.9 g |
| Cholesterol | 164 mg |
| Sodium | 755 mg |

* Percent Daily Values are based on a 2,000 calorie diet.

# CLASSICAL FETTUCCINE

## Ingredients

- 8 oz. dry fettuccine pasta
- 3 cloves garlic
- 1/2 sweet onion, cut into wedges
- 3 tbsps fresh oregano leaves
- 4 tbsps olive oil
- 4 medium tomatoes, diced
- 3 tbsps diced fresh basil
- salt and pepper to taste
- 1 C. spinach leaves
- 1 lb cooked shrimp - peeled and deveined
- 8 oz. fresh mozzarella cheese, diced

## Directions

- Cook your pasta in water and salt for 9 mins then remove all the liquids.
- Pulse the following a few times with a food processor: oregano, onion, and garlic. Once the mix is minced begin to stir fry it in olive oil until everything is browned then add in: the pepper, tomatoes, salt, and basil.
- Let the mix cook for 7 mins.
- Now add in the spinach to the mix and let everything wilt then combine in the shrimp.
- Get everything hot then add in the pasta and the mozzarella and stir the mix. Enjoy.

Amount per serving (4 total)

Timing Information:

| Preparation | 15 m |
|---|---|
| Cooking | 15 m |
| Total Time | 30 m |

Nutritional Information:

| Calories | 651 kcal |
|---|---|
| Fat | 28.5 g |
| Carbohydrates | 52.2g |
| Protein | 43.8 g |
| Cholesterol | 266 mg |
| Sodium | 357 mg |

* Percent Daily Values are based on a 2,000 calorie diet.

# PLUM TOMATO AND OLIVE FILETS

Ingredients

- 5 roma (plum) tomatoes
- 2 tbsps extra virgin olive oil
- 1/2 Spanish onion, diced
- 2 cloves garlic, diced
- 1 pinch Italian seasoning
- 24 kalamata olives, pitted and diced
- 1/4 C. white wine
- 1/4 C. capers
- 1 tsp fresh lemon juice
- 6 leaves fresh basil, diced
- 3 tbsps freshly grated Parmesan cheese
- 1 lb flounder fillets
- 6 leaves fresh basil, torn

Directions

- Set your oven to 425 degrees before doing anything else.
- Get a large pot of water boiling.
- Once the water is boiling add in your tomatoes and let the tomatoes sit in the water for 10 secs then remove them to a bowl of water and ice.
- Once the tomatoes have cooled remove the skins and dice them.
- Now begin to stir fry your onions in olive oil for 7 mins then add in the Italian seasoning, tomatoes, and garlic.

- Let the mix cook for 9 mins then combine in: 1/2 of the basil, olives, lemon juice, wine, and capers.
- Set the heat to low then mix in the parmesan.
- Let the contents cook for 17 mins with a low heat.
- Now place your fish in a casserole dish, pour in the sauce, add the rest of the basil, and put everything in the oven for 14 mins.
- Enjoy.

Amount per serving (4 total)

Timing Information:

| Preparation | 15 m |
|-------------|------|
| Cooking | 30 m |
| Total Time | 45 m |

Nutritional Information:

| Calories | 282 kcal |
|----------|----------|
| Fat | 15.4 g |
| Carbohydrates | 8.2g |
| Protein | 24.4 g |
| Cholesterol | 63 mg |
| Sodium | 777 mg |

* Percent Daily Values are based on a 2,000 calorie diet.

# PINK AND GREEN ITALIAN PASTA

## Ingredients

- 8 oz. dry fettuccine pasta
- 1/4 C. butter
- 1 C. milk
- 1 tbsp all-purpose flour
- 1 C. freshly grated Parmesan cheese
- 1/2 lb smoked salmon, diced
- 1 C. diced fresh spinach
- 2 tbsps capers
- 1/4 C. diced sun-dried tomatoes
- 1/2 C. diced fresh oregano

## Directions

- Boil your pasta in water and salt for 9 mins then remove all the liquid.
- Begin to stir and heat your milk and butter in a large pot then once it is hot add in the flour and get everything thick.
- Slowly add in the parmesan and continue heating it until the cheese melts.
- Break the fish into the parmesan mix then add: the oregano, spinach, sun-dried tomatoes, and capers.
- Let the mix simmer for 5 mins while stirring.
- Lay your pasta on a serving plate then liberally top it with the buttery sauce. Enjoy.

Amount per serving (4 total)

Timing Information:

| Preparation | 15 m |
|---|---|
| Cooking | 25 m |
| Total Time | 40 m |

Nutritional Information:

| Calories | 512 kcal |
|---|---|
| Fat | 22.6 g |
| Carbohydrates | 49.4g |
| Protein | 28.9 g |
| Cholesterol | 66 mg |
| Sodium | 1065 mg |

* Percent Daily Values are based on a 2,000 calorie diet.

# CORNMEAL PARMESAN COD FILETS

## Ingredients

- 1/4 C. fine dry bread crumbs
- 2 tbsps grated Parmesan cheese
- 1 tbsp cornmeal
- 1 tsp olive oil
- 1/2 tsp Italian seasoning
- 1/8 tsp garlic powder
- 1/8 tsp ground black pepper
- 4 (3 oz.) fillets cod fillets
- 1 egg white, lightly beaten

## Directions

- Set your oven to 450 degrees before doing anything else.
- Get a bowl, combine: pepper, bread crumbs, garlic powder, cheese, Italian spice, oil, and cornmeal.
- Get a broiling pan and coat the rack with nonstick spray.
- Layer your fish then coat it with egg whites.
- Now evenly divide your crumb mix over the fish and cook everything in the oven for 11 mins.
- Enjoy.

Amount per serving (4 total)

Timing Information:

| | |
|---|---|
| Preparation | 15 m |
| Cooking | 10 m |
| Total Time | 25 m |

Nutritional Information:

| | |
|---|---|
| Calories | 131 kcal |
| Fat | 2.9 g |
| Carbohydrates | 7g |
| Protein | 18.1 g |
| Cholesterol | 39 mg |
| Sodium | 148 mg |

* Percent Daily Values are based on a 2,000 calorie diet.

# MAGGIE'S EASY PUTTANESCA

# (SOUTHERN ITALIAN STYLE)

Ingredients

- 8 oz. pasta
- 1/2 C. olive oil
- 3 cloves garlic, minced
- 2 C. diced tomatoes, pushed through a sieve
- 4 anchovy filets, rinsed and diced
- 2 tbsps tomato paste
- 3 tbsps capers
- 20 Greek olives, pitted and coarsely diced
- 1/2 tsp crushed red pepper flakes

Directions

- Boil your pasta in water and salt for 9 mins then remove all the liquids.
- Now being to stir fry your garlic in oil until it is browned all over.
- Then add the tomatoes and cook the mix for 7 mins before adding in: the pepper flakes, anchovies, olives, tomato paste, and capers.
- Let the mix cook for 12 mins and stir everything at least 2 times.
- Now add in the pasta and stir everything to evenly coat the noodles.
- Enjoy.

Amount per serving (4 total)

Timing Information:

| Preparation | 25 m |
|---|---|
| Cooking | 15 m |
| Total Time | 40 m |

Nutritional Information:

| Calories | 490 kcal |
|---|---|
| Fat | 34 g |
| Carbohydrates | 38.7g |
| Protein | 9.3 g |
| Cholesterol | 44 mg |
| Sodium | 728 mg |

* Percent Daily Values are based on a 2,000 calorie diet.

# ITALIAN STYLE COD

Ingredients

- 2 tbsps olive oil
- 1 onion, thinly sliced
- 2 cloves garlic, minced
- 1 (14.5 oz.) can diced tomatoes
- 1/2 C. black olives, pitted and sliced
- 1 tbsp diced fresh parsley
- 1/2 C. dry white wine
- 1 lb cod fillets

Directions

- Stir fry your garlic and onions in olive oil until tender then combine in: wine, tomatoes, parsley, and olives.
- Let the mix gently boil for 7 mins then add in the cod.
- Let the cod gently cook for 7 more mins until it is fully done.
- Enjoy.

Amount per serving (4 total)

Timing Information:

| Preparation | 10 m |
|---|---|
| Cooking | 15 m |
| Total Time | 25 m |

Nutritional Information:

| Calories | 230 kcal |
|---|---|
| Fat | 9.4 g |
| Carbohydrates | 8.2g |
| Protein | 21.2 g |
| Cholesterol | 41 mg |
| Sodium | 459 mg |

* Percent Daily Values are based on a 2,000 calorie diet.

# Easy Restaurant Style Clams

Ingredients

- 1/2 C. butter
- 5 cloves garlic, minced
- 2 C. dry white wine
- 1 tbsp dried oregano
- 1 tbsp dried parsley
- 1 tsp crushed red pepper flakes (optional)
- 36 clams in shell, scrubbed

Directions

- Stir fry your garlic in butter for 60 secs then add in the pepper flakes, wine, parsley, and oregano.
- Stir the mix then add in the clams.
- Place a lid on the pan and let everything cook until the clams have opened.
- Divide the mix between serving bowls.
- Enjoy.

Amount per serving (6 total)

Timing Information:

| Preparation | 15 m |
|---|---|
| Cooking | 15 m |
| Total Time | 30 m |

Nutritional Information:

| Calories | 227 kcal |
|---|---|
| Fat | 15.7 g |
| Carbohydrates | 4.4g |
| Protein | 3.2 g |
| Cholesterol | 47 mg |
| Sodium | 126 mg |

* Percent Daily Values are based on a 2,000 calorie diet.

# Romano Roughy

Ingredients

- 1/4 C. Italian seasoned bread crumbs
- 2 tbsps grated Parmesan cheese
- 2 tbsps grated Romano cheese
- 1/4 tsp garlic powder
- 1/2 tsp salt, or to taste
- 1 lb orange roughy fillets
- 1/4 C. butter, melted
- 1 tbsp diced fresh parsley

Directions

- Spray a casserole dish with nonstick spray then set your oven to 400 degrees before doing anything else.
- Get a bowl, combine: salt, bread crumbs, garlic powder, parmesan, and Romano.
- Coat your filets with butter then coat them with the crumb mix.
- Place everything into the casserole dish and top them with parsley.
- Cook the fish in the oven for 14 mins.
- Enjoy.

Amount per serving (4 total)

Timing Information:

| Preparation | 15 m |
|---|---|
| Cooking | 15 m |
| Total Time | 30 m |

Nutritional Information:

| Calories | 242 kcal |
|---|---|
| Fat | 14.4 g |
| Carbohydrates | 5.4g |
| Protein | 21.9 g |
| Cholesterol | 105 mg |
| Sodium | 645 mg |

* Percent Daily Values are based on a 2,000 calorie diet.

# CLASSICAL PENNE PASTA

Ingredients

- 1 (16 oz.) package penne pasta
- 2 tbsps olive oil
- 1/4 C. diced red onion
- 1 tbsp diced garlic
- 1/4 C. white wine
- 2 (14.5 oz.) cans diced tomatoes
- 1 lb shrimp, peeled and deveined
- 1 C. grated Parmesan cheese

Directions

- Boil your pasta in water and salt for 9 mins then remove the liquids.
- Now begin to stir fry your garlic and onions in oil until the onions are soft.
- Then add in the tomatoes and wine.
- Simmer the mix for 12 mins while stirring. Then add in the shrimp and cook everything for 6 mins.
- Now add the pasta and stir everything to evenly coat the noodles.
- Enjoy.

Amount per serving (8 total)

Timing Information:

| Preparation | 10 m |
|---|---|
| Cooking | 25 m |
| Total Time | 35 m |

Nutritional Information:

| Calories | 385 kcal |
|---|---|
| Fat | 8.5 g |
| Carbohydrates | 48.5g |
| Protein | 24.5 g |
| Cholesterol | 95 mg |
| Sodium | 399 mg |

* Percent Daily Values are based on a 2,000 calorie diet.

# Parmesan Orzo

Ingredients

- 1/2 C. butter, divided
- 8 pearl onions
- 1 C. uncooked orzo pasta
- 1/2 C. sliced fresh mushrooms
- 1 C. water
- 1/2 C. white wine
- garlic powder to taste
- salt and pepper to taste
- 1/2 C. grated Parmesan cheese
- 1/4 C. fresh parsley

Directions

- Stir fry your onions in half of the butter until it is browned then add in the rest of the butter, mushrooms, and the orzo.
- Continue frying everything for 7 mins.
- Now combine in the wine and the water and get everything boiling.
- Once the mix is boiling, set the heat to low, and cook everything for 9 mins after adding in the pepper, salt and garlic powder.
- Once the orzo is done top it with parsley and parmesan.
- Enjoy.

Amount per serving (6 total)

Timing Information:

| Preparation | 15 m |
|---|---|
| Cooking | 25 m |
| Total Time | 40 m |

Nutritional Information:

| Calories | 327 kcal |
|---|---|
| Fat | 18.6 g |
| Carbohydrates | 28.1g |
| Protein | 8.6 g |
| Cholesterol | 48 mg |
| Sodium | 306 mg |

* Percent Daily Values are based on a 2,000 calorie diet.

# GARLIC AND ASPARAGUS STIR FRY

Ingredients

- 1/4 C. butter
- 2 tbsps olive oil
- 1 tsp coarse salt
- 1/4 tsp ground black pepper
- 3 cloves garlic, minced
- 1 lb fresh asparagus spears, trimmed

Directions

- Begin to stir fry your garlic in olive oil and butter. Then add in some pepper and salt.
- Let the garlic fry for 60 secs then add in the asparagus and fry them for 12 mins.
- Enjoy.

Amount per serving (4 total)

Timing Information:

| Preparation | 5 m |
|---|---|
| Cooking | 15 m |
| Total Time | 25 m |

Nutritional Information:

| Calories | 188 kcal |
|---|---|
| Fat | 18.4 g |
| Carbohydrates | 5.2g |
| Protein | 2.8 g |
| Cholesterol | 31 mg |
| Sodium | 525 mg |

* Percent Daily Values are based on a 2,000 calorie diet.

# Pasta Rustic

Ingredients

- 1 lb farfalle (bow tie) pasta
- 1/3 C. olive oil
- 1 clove garlic, chopped
- 1/4 C. butter
- 2 small zucchini, quartered and sliced
- 1 onion, chopped
- 1 tomato, chopped
- 1 (8 oz) package mushrooms, sliced
- 1 tbsp dried oregano
- 1 tbsp paprika
- salt and pepper to taste

Directions

- Boil your pasta for 10 mins in water and salt. Remove excess liquid and set aside.
- Fry your salt, pepper, garlic, paprika, zucchini, oregano, mushrooms, onion, and tomato, for 17 mins in olive oil.
- Mix the veggies and pasta.
- Enjoy.

Servings: 4 servings

Timing Information:

| Preparation | Cooking | Total Time |
|---|---|---|
| 10 mins | 25 mins | 35 mins |

Nutritional Information:

| Calories | 717 kcal |
|---|---|
| Carbohydrates | 92.8 g |
| Cholesterol | 31 mg |
| Fat | 32.9 g |
| Fiber | 7.5 g |
| Protein | 18.1 g |
| Sodium | 491 mg |

* Percent Daily Values are based on a 2,000 calorie diet.

# Panettone Bread

# (Sweet Dessert Bread with Fruit)

## Ingredients

- 1/3 C. warm water
- 2 (.25 oz.) packages active dry yeast
- 4 C. all-purpose flour
- 1/2 C. warm milk
- 2/3 C. white sugar
- 4 eggs
- 2 egg yolks
- 1 tsp vanilla extract
- 12 tbsps unsalted butter
- 2 C. candied mixed fruit
- 2 1/2 tsps grated lemon zest
- 2 tbsps orange zest
- 2 tbsps butter, melted
- 1 egg yolk
- 1 tbsp cream

## Directions

- Get a bowl and run it under hot water. Once the bowl is warm add your warm water and top the water with 1 pack of yeast.
- Leave this mix until the yeast has dissolved then combine in 1/2 C. of flour.
- Place a covering of plastic around the bowl and let the mix sit for 40 mins.

- Now add the rest of the yeast over warm and milk and let it sit until the yeast has dissolved.
- Get a 3rd bowl, combine: vanilla, sugar, egg yolks, and eggs. Combine this mix with the milk and yeast mix.
- Now add in the contents of the first bowl and mix everything together.
- Get a 4th bowl, combine: 1.5 C. flour and butter.
- Mix everything until crumbly. Then gradually add in the eggs.
- Mix everything with an electric mixer on high speed for 5 mins.
- Now add in your zest and fruits.
- Place the dough in an oiled bowl and turn it. Place a covering of plastic on the bowl and let the dough rise for 4 hrs.
- Now lay out three bags.
- Roll the bags down and coat them with melted butter. Once the dough is finish rising break it into 3 pieces and knead the dough into 3 balls and place each ball in a bag.
- Layer your bags on a cookie sheet and let the bread rise for 3 more hrs.
- Now set your oven to 400 degrees before doing anything else. Create two diagonally incisions on the top of each loaf and coat each one with a mix of cream and egg yolk.
- Remove the dough from the bags and cook them in the oven for 10 mins then set the heat to 375 degrees and cook for 35 more mins.
- Enjoy.

Amount per serving (36 total)

Timing Information:

| Preparation | 10 m |
| Cooking | 5 h |
| Total Time | 5 h 10 m |

Nutritional Information:

| Calories | 153 kcal |
| Fat | 5.8 g |
| Carbohydrates | 22.9g |
| Protein | 2.7 g |
| Cholesterol | 50 mg |
| Sodium | 16 mg |

* Percent Daily Values are based on a 2,000 calorie diet.

# THANKS FOR READING! NOW LET'S TRY SOME **SUSHI** AND **DUMP DINNERS**....

Send the Book!

To grab this **box set** simply follow the link mentioned above, or tap the book cover.

This will take you to a page where you can simply enter your email address and a PDF version of the **box set** will be emailed to you.

I hope you are ready for some serious cooking!

Send the Book!

You will also receive updates about all my new books when they are free.

Also don't forget to like and subscribe on the social networks. I love meeting my readers. Links to all my profiles are below so please click and connect : )

Facebook

Twitter

# Come On...
# Let's Be Friends : )

I adore my readers and love connecting with them socially. Please follow the links below so we can connect on Facebook, Twitter, and Google+.

Facebook

Twitter

I also have a blog that I regularly update for my readers so check it out below.

My Blog

# CAN I ASK A FAVOUR?

If you found this book interesting, or have otherwise found any benefit in it. Then may I ask that you post a review of it on Amazon? Nothing excites me more than new reviews, especially reviews which suggest new topics for writing. I do read all reviews and I always factor feedback into my newer works.

So if you are willing to take ten minutes to write what you sincerely thought about this book then please visit our Amazon page and post your opinions.

Again thank you!

# Interested in Other Easy Cookbooks?

Everything is easy! Check out my Amazon Author page for more great cookbooks:

*For a complete listing of all my books please see my author page.*

Printed in Great Britain
by Amazon